STEP
FORWARD
WITH
GRIT

SHANNON WELBOURN

Crabtree Publishing Company
www.crabtreebooks.com

STEP FORWARD!

Author
Shannon Welbourn

Series research and development
Reagan Miller

Editorial director
Kathy Middleton

Editors
Reagan Miller, Janine Deschenes

Series Consultant
Larry Miller: BA (Sociology), BPE, MSc.Ed
Retired teacher, guidance counselor, and certified coach

Print and production coordinator
Katherine Berti

Design and photo research
Katherine Berti

Photographs
AP Images: Sputnik, p 17
iStock: ©shironosov, p 11; ©Christopher Futcher, p 13;
Shutterstock: ©Juriah Mosin, p 14
Other images by Shutterstock

Library and Archives Canada Cataloguing in Publication

Welbourn, Shannon, author
    Step forward with grit / Shannon Welbourn.

(Step forward!)
Includes index.
Issued in print and electronic formats.
ISBN 978-0-7787-2767-5 (hardback).--
ISBN 978-0-7787-2790-3 (paperback).--
ISBN 978-1-4271-1825-7 (html)

    1. Resilience (Personality trait)--Juvenile literature.
2. Persistence--Juvenile literature. I. Title.

BF698.35.R47W45 2016   j155.2'4   C2016-903349-X
                                            C2016-903350-3

Library of Congress Cataloging-in-Publication Data

Names: Welbourn, Shannon, author.
Title: Step forward with grit / Shannon Welbourn.
Description: New York : Crabtree Publishing Company, [2017] |
    Series: Step forward! | Includes index.
Identifiers: LCCN 2016034713 (print) | LCCN 2016043365 (ebook) |
    ISBN 9780778727675 (reinforced library binding : alk. paper) |
    ISBN 9780778727903 (pbk. : alk. paper) |
    ISBN 9781427118257 (Electronic HTML)
Subjects: LCSH: Determination (Personality trait) in children--Juvenile
    literature. | Determination (Personality trait)--Juvenile literature.
Classification: LCC BF698.35.D48 W45 2017 (print) | LCC BF698.35.D48 (ebook)
    | DDC 155.2/32--dc23
LC record available at https://lccn.loc.gov/2016034713

Crabtree Publishing Company

www.crabtreebooks.com   1-800-387-7650

Printed in Canada/102016/IH20160811

Published in Canada
Crabtree Publishing
616 Welland Ave.
St. Catharines, Ontario
L2M 5V6

Published in the United States
Crabtree Publishing
PMB 59051
350 Fifth Avenue, 59th Floor
New York, New York 10118

Published in the United Kingdom
Crabtree Publishing
Maritime House
Basin Road North, Hove
BN41 1WR

Published in Australia
Crabtree Publishing
3 Charles Street
Coburg North
VIC 3058

CONTENTS

WHAT IS GRIT?

Can you think about a time in your life when you became discouraged, or felt like giving up? Did you find a way to finish what you started? Or were you stopped in your tracks?

Grit is a **mindset** that includes the character qualities of **persistence** and **determination**. It is also being **resilient** and strong despite any obstacles that you encounter. People with grit finish what they start and resist giving up. Everyone has the ability to develop grit.

Each time things don't go exactly how we want, we have an opportunity. We can feel discouraged and sad, or we can show our strength and determination. How we learn and grow from these challenges helps us to develop grit. Each time we fail and try again, our grit becomes stronger.

The challenges we face can become opportunities to build grit.

STEP FURTHER

What is something in your life that could benefit from a gritty attitude?

GRIT GROWS GOALS!

Grit helps you to succeed in different parts of your life.

When you set out to do something, you have a goal in mind. A goal is something you want to achieve. Sometimes we are successful on our first try. Other times, it takes many tries to reach our goal. Failing and having the determination to keep trying until you reach your goal is what makes you gritty. Grit can take time to develop. You will work on building grit throughout your life.

You grow and develop each time you do not reach your goal but decide to try again. This is called **perseverance**. When you try again, you get stronger and more resilient. Each time you try, you learn more about who you are. Learning to be gritty is important, so don't give up!

We build grit each time we fall down and get back up.

CLIMAX-FISHER KNIGHTS

Name: Climax-Fisher Knights

From: Fisher, Minnesota

Accomplishment: Didn't give up and accomplished their goal...on the 85th try!

The girls' basketball team from Climax-Fisher High School is an amazing example of grit.

The team had been on a losing streak from 2011 to 2014. Over the years, they had lost a total of 84 games straight! But that did not stop the coach from inspiring the players, and it did not stop the girls from trying their hardest. The players showed their love for the game. They displayed grit by working together as a team and not giving up. Even in the 85th game, when five players **fouled out** and only three players were left on the court, they didn't give up. The Knights stuck together and believed in each other. The game went into double overtime and the girls won the game, breaking the 84-game losing streak!

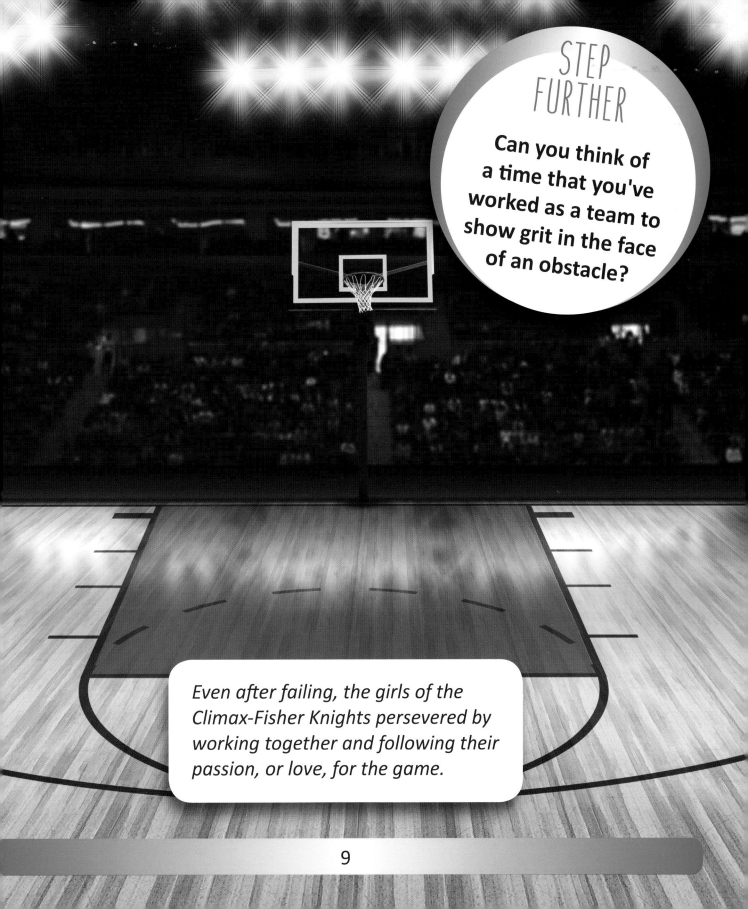

STEP FURTHER

Can you think of a time that you've worked as a team to show grit in the face of an obstacle?

Even after failing, the girls of the Climax-Fisher Knights persevered by working together and following their passion, or love, for the game.

GRIT AT HOME

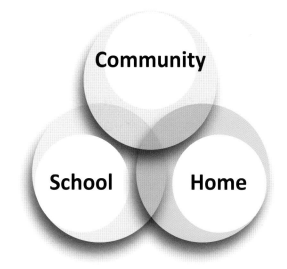

Community

School

Home

Can you think of a time that you used grit at home? Family members can all work together to build grit.

Families sometimes have to take on big tasks together. You and your family are spending a weekend cleaning out the garage. There are a lot of old toys and tools in there! You'd rather be spending the weekend playing with friends, but you made a **commitment** to help clean the garage and your family is counting on you.

Even though cleaning out the garage is a difficult job, you show grit when you stick with your commitment and help your family finish the task. When everyone works together to get things finished, you show grit as a family!

Following through to finish what you start helps build grit. It also shows others that they can depend on you.

GRIT AT SCHOOL

Community

School

Home

At school, we can build grit every day. By persevering to work hard even when things are difficult, we develop grit and succeed at school.

We can be faced with many challenges throughout the day at school. Most kids find schoolwork difficult from time to time, especially when they are learning something new. Think about a time that you felt frustrated learning something new. You might have felt like giving up, but it's important to persevere and keep trying. Even though you might get the wrong answer sometimes, trying again builds grit at school.

You're working on a project with a partner in science class. You need to build a model bridge that can hold up a 5-pound (2.3 kg) weight. Every time you test your bridge, the weight falls through! It could be easy to feel discouraged, but you and your partner decide to keep trying different designs for the bridge until one works. When you keep trying, you learn how to figure out problems and you develop grit.

*Showing grit means trying different **strategies** until you get it right.*

GRIT IN YOUR COMMUNITY

Community

School **Home**

A community is a group of people who live, work, and play in a place. Your home, school, and neighborhood are part of your community.

You can show and build grit in your community in many different ways. You could build grit by helping to clean up the local park every Saturday or growing flowers in a community garden—even if they wilt when it's too hot outside.

You might decide to run in a race for charity. You can show your determination by spending the weeks before the race raising money for the charity. Then, you complete the race even when it gets hard and you feel tired. That's true grit!

Maybe you are part of the baseball team in your community. You set a goal for yourself to make one run every game. Setting a goal for yourself can help you build grit because even when you face challenges, your goal can keep you focused. Grit helps you to keep going until you reach your goal.

> "I can accept failure. Everyone fails at something. But I can't accept not trying again."
>
> —Michael Jordan
> Pro basketball player

Keep trying. Keep practicing. Your results will show your hard work and grit.

ABDUL MUQEET

At the age of 8, Abdul Muqeet learned that plastic bags cause serious pollution. Passionate about helping the environment, Abdul has used his unstoppable grit to help stop the use of plastic bags.

Name: Abdul Muqeet

From: Abu Dhabi, United Arab Emirates

Accomplishment: Followed his passion for the environment to help get rid of plastic bags

When Abdul's teacher announced that his class would be having a "no plastic day" in October 2010, Abdul decided to learn why he should avoid using plastic. He discovered that plastic can be harmful to the environment, and decided he would work to fix the problem. Abdul decided to create bags out of paper instead of plastic to help stop people in his community from using plastic bags when shopping. He worked very hard to make the bags himself out of recycled newspaper.

Although it took time, Abdul did not give up on his goal. Many years later, Abdul still follows his passion to save the environment and solve pollution problems in his country and around the world. He uses his grit to continue to make paper bags and encourage recycling. With a little creativity and a lot of grit, Abdul is inspiring people everywhere to live in a more environmentally friendly way.

Abdul has made over 6,000 paper shopping bags over the last several years! He has been nicknamed "The Paper Bag Boy."

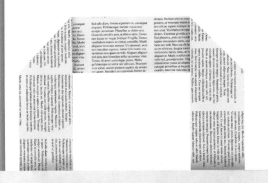

"A small step in our day-to-day life can make a big difference to the environment. It is our sole responsibility to care for Planet Earth and make it a better place to live."

—Abdul Muqeet

OVERCOMING CHALLENGES

Having grit comes down to a mindset. Your thoughts and actions are what build grit.

Think of the well-known quote— "If at first you don't succeed, try, try again." When something doesn't go your way, don't give up. When you need a bit of grit to help you succeed, try these tips:

• Sometimes we can lose focus or get discouraged. But don't let this be an **obstacle**! Remember your goals and why they matter to you to help you keep trying.

• Look at what you are doing and review your plan of action. Should you try a different strategy?

• Learn each time and adjust your strategies as needed. Each attempt should get you closer to your goal.

STEP FURTHER

What advice would you give someone who experienced failure?

Sometimes you have to fail in order to succeed. Think about a time you did not reach your goal. How did this make you feel? You are in control of how you let failure affect you. Should you get discouraged and give up, or use it as a way to learn, improve, and try again? You can learn to look at failures as challenges, and view challenges as opportunities. This will help you develop a gritty mindset.

ENCOURAGING GRIT IN OTHERS

Once you have figured out how to develop your gritty mindset, you can help others too!

Encourage others to build their mindset for grit as well. If you see someone showing grit, encourage them to keep going. When you see someone fail or get discouraged, you can encourage grit by cheering them on! Encourage them to not give up. Show others how to persevere by working hard to achieve your goals, no matter the challenges in your way. Encourage others to keep positive and to show determination. When you believe in something, it is easier to keep going. You have to believe you can do it—even when others may not. Help others to see that they have grit too! Be gritty!

When you show others that you believe in them, you are helping them to believe in themselves. That builds grit!

STEPPING FORWARD

Grit can help you reach your goals now and in the future!

To keep your grit on track, pay attention to your thoughts and actions and make sure they support a gritty mindset. Use the statements and images below to help you see the ways you show grit and areas where you can work to build more grit in your life. There are no right or wrong answers. Use this page again and again in the future to help make sure you keep stepping forward with grit!

Read each statement. How well does it describe you?
Think about your recent thoughts and actions to help you decide.

I finish what I am working on before starting something new.	I can give a lot of effort and time to things that I think are interesting and important.	I can deal with setbacks and obstacles. I don't get too discouraged or give up.	When I make a mistake, I think about what I can learn from it.	I use ma different strategie to reach my goals

Very much like me

Somewhat like me

Not like me at all

LEARNING MORE

BOOKS

Jordan, Deloris. *Salt in His Shoes: Michael Jordan in Pursuit of a Dream.* Simon & Schuster Books for Young Readers, 2003.

Morganelli, Adrianna. *Wilma Rudolph: Track and Field Champion.* Crabtree Publishing, 2016.

Neimark, Jill. *The Hugging Tree: A Story About Resilience.* Magination Press, 2015.

WEBSITES

www.bit.ly/amigritty
This website includes a scale made up of 12 questions to help you discover how gritty you are.

www.characterlab.org/tools/grit
A site promoting character development in students.

www.ted.com
Search for "grit" or "Angela Lee Duckworth" for the inspiring TED Talk "Grit: The power of passion and perseverance."

WORDS TO KNOW

attitude [AT-i-tood] noun A feeling, mood, or way of thinking
benefit [BEN-uh-fit] noun An advantage or something that is good
commitment [kuh-MIT-muh nt] noun A promise to do something
determination [dih-tur-muh-NEY-shuhn] noun The quality of being firm, or having strength of mind and character
fouled out [fowl-ed out] verb In basketball, to be removed from a game after committing too many fouls against other players
mindset [MAHYND-set] noun An intention, attitude, or mood
obstacle [OB-stuh-kuhl] noun Something that gets in the way
perseverance [pur-suh-VEER-uhns] noun Persistence in a course of action despite difficulties
persistence [per-SIS-tuh ns] noun Determined continuance of action
resilient [ri-ZIL-yuhnt] adjective Recovering or springing back after a challenge
strategy (STRAT-i-jee) noun A plan for achieving a goal

INDEX

ABOUT THE AUTHOR

Shannon Welbourn is a freelance author of educational K-12 books. She holds an honors BA in Child & Youth Studies, and is a certified teacher. Shannon works full-time as a Library and Media Specialist. In this position, she works closely with teachers and teacher candidates, helping to inspire and develop a passion for learning. Shannon lives close to Niagara Falls and enjoys vacationing in the Muskokas with her family.